Mile

C000135657

Miles Guide To Corfu 2024

A journey into the heart of the ionian

Contents

Introduction

Corfu is an island of exceptional beauty and charm, where verdant hills meet grand residences and serene beaches meet notable museums, offering distinct experiences for every visitor.

The heart of the island, Corfu Town, is a treasure trove of history, shaped by Venetian, French, and British influences. It invites visitors to wander and ponder, with its narrow stone alleys known as "kandouni," prestigious museums like the Museum of Asian Art, and the bustling Liston promenade. The town is a vibrant letter from the past, with its stately palaces, refined homes, and inviting plazas.

Moving beyond the town's energy, Corfu reveals a world filled with charming coastal villages, lush islets, luxurious resorts, and wild landscapes. The seamless fusion of such varied elements is indeed noteworthy.

Leaving the city noise behind, Corfu offers a variety of experiences. Small, picturesque fishing villages live in harmony with the sea. There are pockets of paradise where greenery flourishes, tiny islands that seem to float on the azure waters, and opulent hotels offering every conceivable comfort. Additionally, there are areas of untouched nature, inviting the adventurous to explore.

These distinct parts, each with its unique charm, come together to form the grand story of Corfu. It is a place where the lines between man-made and natural beauty blur, where luxury lives alongside simplicity, and where every corner holds the promise of a new discovery. The island's seamless blend of sights, sounds, and sensations is truly remarkable.

From the engaging charm of Corfu Town to the outskirts of the island, where stunning beaches await, Corfu's shores, with their golden sands, lush greenery, and towering cliffs, rank among Greece's most beautiful. Beaches like Dassia, Paleokastritsa, Glyfada, Kontokali, and Kavos beckon with their allure.

For those seeking history and culture, Corfu's landmarks are ready to enchant. Highlights include the Achillion Palace, once a retreat for Austria's Princess Sissi, and Mon Repos Palace, the birthplace of Prince Philip. Must-see sites like the charming Panagia Vlacherna and the legendary Mouse Island will deepen one's appreciation for Corfu.

The culinary journey is equally thrilling. Corfu's cuisine, a feast of meats, seafood, pasta, and herbs, promises to delight food enthusiasts. The island's outstanding restaurants and cozy taverns serve the best local fare.

Corfu offers a warm invitation—a destination that is undeniably alluring.Corfu is an island of exceptional beauty and charm, where verdant hills meet grand residences and serene beaches meet notable museums, offering distinct experiences for every visitor.

The heart of the island, Corfu Town, is a treasure trove of history, shaped by Venetian, French, and British influences. It invites visitors to wander and ponder, with its narrow stone alleys known as "kandouni," prestigious museums like the Museum of Asian Art, and the bustling Liston promenade. The town is a vibrant letter from the past, with its stately palaces, refined homes, and inviting plazas.

Moving beyond the town's energy, Corfu reveals a world filled with charming coastal villages, lush islets, luxurious resorts, and wild landscapes. The seamless fusion of such varied elements is indeed noteworthy.

Leaving the city noise behind, Corfu offers a variety of experiences. Small, picturesque fishing villages live in harmony with the sea. There are pockets of paradise where greenery flourishes, tiny islands that seem to float on the azure waters, and opulent hotels offering every conceivable comfort. Additionally, there are areas of untouched nature, inviting the adventurous to explore.

These distinct parts, each with its unique charm, come together to form the grand story of Corfu. It is a place where the lines between man-made and natural beauty blur, where luxury lives alongside simplicity, and where every corner holds the promise of a new discovery. The island's seamless blend of sights, sounds, and sensations is truly remarkable.

From the engaging charm of Corfu Town to the outskirts of the island, where stunning beaches await, Corfu's shores, with their golden sands, lush greenery, and towering cliffs, rank among Greece's most beautiful. Beaches like Dassia, Paleokastritsa, Glyfada, Kontokali, and Kavos beckon with their allure.

For those seeking history and culture, Corfu's landmarks are ready to enchant. Highlights include the Achillion Palace, once a retreat for Austria's

Princess Sissi, and Mon Repos Palace, the birthplace of Prince Philip. Must-see sites like the charming Panagia Vlacherna and the legendary Mouse Island will deepen one's appreciation for Corfu.

The culinary journey is equally thrilling. Corfu's cuisine, a feast of meats, seafood, pasta, and herbs, promises to delight food enthusiasts. The island's outstanding restaurants and cozy taverns serve the best local fare.

Corfu offers a warm invitation—a destination that is undeniably alluring.

Geography And Location

Corfu may not be as large as Kefalonia, but it is a significant island in its own merit, spanning 588 square kilometers. It is celebrated for its extensive coastline of about 217 kilometers, known for its pristine beaches with fine sand and clear waters. The northern coast of Corfu is marked by its rugged landscape, steeped in historical importance and wild beauty, especially notable in places like Paleokastritsa.

The island's landscape is clearly segmented into three areas by the Pantokrator and Saint Decca (Agioi Deka) mountain ranges. The north is mountainous, the center is a mix of valleys and hills, and the south consists of large areas of flat, arable land suitable for farming. Mount Pantokrator, the tallest peak on the island, reaches a height of 911 meters. Near the entrance to the port, one can find two small islands, Lazareto and Vidos (or Ptychia), located between Corfu Bay and Gouvia Bay.

Corfu's geography is also characterized by two lakes and four rivers that tend to dry up in the dry summer months but are replenished during the rainy winter season. The island is known for receiving the most rainfall in Greece, which contributes to its exceptionally fertile soil, supporting the extensive olive groves in the northern part of the island.

Moreover, the small island of Mathraki, covering just three square kilometers, is part of the Diapontia Islands, a group of three islands in the northern Ionian Sea. A short 45-minute boat ride from Corfu, Mathraki, along with Ereikoussa and Othoni, provides a tranquil escape from the bustle of the larger island.

History

Corfu, also known as Kérkyra to the Greeks, is an island rich in history.

Legends and Lore: The earliest narratives of Corfu are shrouded in myth. According to legend, it was the dwelling of the Phaeacians, where the epic hero Odysseus was cast ashore and encountered Nausicaa, as depicted in Homer's Odyssey. The appellation 'Corfu' is derived from the Greek term 'koryphaios', alluding to the prominent peaks of its ancient fortress.

Early History: The annals of Corfu's history trace back to around 734 BCE with the arrival of settlers from Corinth. The island rose to prominence as a maritime power, frequently conflicting with Corinth. Its advantageous position in the Mediterranean rendered it an attractive conquest for various rulers.

Middle Ages and Venetian Influence: Advancing to the medieval era, Corfu faced numerous assaults yet retained its autonomy. The Venetian rule, which spanned four centuries starting in the 1400s, left a lasting legacy, with formidable castles still standing today.

Under French and British Rule, and Joining Greece: Following the decline of Venetian authority, the French and then the British assumed control over Corfu, each imparting their distinctive influences on the island's culture and lifestyle. In 1864, Corfu was annexed to the newly established Greek state, marking the beginning of a new epoch.

Corfu Today: In contemporary times, Corfu represents a confluence of its varied historical influences, boasting a flourishing culture in music, arts, and gastronomy. The spirit of history resonates through the narrow lanes of the old town, and the island's essence is as enduring as the Mediterranean sun.

This brief overview of Corfu's history is merely an introduction. For visitors, the island serves as a veritable open-air museum, with each corner narrating stories of conflict, endurance, and allure. Corfu has long been a junction for diverse cultures, each contributing to the island's unique and enchanting aura.

To gain a comprehensive understanding of Corfu, one might visit its historical landmarks, museums, and libraries, where the island's narrative is meticulously preserved for educational and inspirational purposes. Thus, Corfu stands as a testament to the convergence of historical and contemporary worlds, forging an island teeming with life and narratives.

Climate And Weather

Corfu is widely recognized for its welcoming environment, reminiscent of the comfort found in the presence of a cherished friend.

In the summer, from June through August, the island is vibrant with days marked by clear skies and the sun's radiance. The temperature generally remains in the lower 30s Celsius, which is in the 80s Fahrenheit, creating perfect conditions for beach outings or coastal sailing. As dusk falls, the air cools, offering a pleasant atmosphere for leisurely evenings at seaside cafes.

During the winter months, from December to February, Corfu settles into a peaceful pace. The mercury falls to a range of 10 to 15 degrees Celsius, or 50 to 59 degrees Fahrenheit. While rain is more common, it typically manifests as short showers that only serve to accentuate the lush greenery of the island's landscape.

The transitional seasons of spring and autumn are perhaps Corfu's most understated periods, providing a break from the bustle of tourists while still enjoying temperate weather. Temperatures hover between 15 to 25 degrees Celsius, or 59 to 77 degrees Fahrenheit. Despite the occasional rainfall, there are ample sunny days to enjoy. These seasons are perfect for those who wish to discover the island's natural paths or historic routes without the full force of summer's warmth.

No matter the season, Corfu's climate is integral to its appeal. The island's charm is defined by the gentle warmth of the sun, the soothing sea breezes, and the inviting Mediterranean ambiance. A visit to Corfu offers an opportunity to revel in its pleasant climate, ensuring an unforgettable experience.

PART 1 : PLANNING YOUR JOURNEY TO THE ISLE OF CORFU

How To Get To Corfu

Arrival by Air:

Corfu is accessible via the Ioannis Kapodistrias International Airport, conveniently located near Corfu Town. Year-round flights are available, with an increased frequency during the summer months when direct connections from over 20 cities are established.

Athens to Corfu: Direct flights operate throughout the year, typically lasting 70 minutes. The summer season sees additional flights. Airlines servicing this route include Aegean Airlines, Olympic Air, Sky Express, and RyanAir.

Thessaloniki to Corfu: In the summer, daily flights are available from Thessaloniki, with a duration of approximately 60 minutes, operated by the same carriers as the Athens route.

International Connections:Note that international flights are predominantly seasonal, with schedules subject to change during the summer period.

Arrival by Sea:

Alternatively, Corfu can be reached by ferry, with departures from Igoumenitsa and Patra on the Greek mainland.

Igoumenitsa to Corfu: Ferries operate daily, with a higher frequency in the summer, and the crossing takes about 1.5 hours. Services run from early morning until late evening.

Patra to Corfu: A less frequent service, with two ferries weekly, the journey from Patra spans approximately 7.5 hours.

From Italy: Travelers from Italy can embark on a ferry from Bari or Ancona, an ideal option for those journeying from central Europe and wishing to transport their vehicle.

Ferries also connect Corfu to the neighboring Paxi and Diapontia Islands, especially during the summer months.

Whether by air or sea, multiple travel options are available for those planning a visit to the enchanting island of Corfu. Select the mode of transportation that aligns with your preferences and prepare for a memorable adventure.

ROUTES TO CORFU

Corfu, an island with a population of approximately 100,000, maintains robust sea connectivity throughout the year. The island's ferry services facilitate travel to the mainland at Igoumenitsa and to adjacent smaller islands. Additionally, maritime connections extend to three Italian cities: Ancona, Bari, and Venice.

It is essential to acknowledge that ferry schedules are subject to annual revisions, with most operators publishing their timetables in March. Subsequent to their release, reservations for ferry journeys can be made through an online booking platform.

Igoumenitsa serves as the primary access point to Corfu for travelers originating from the mainland. Situated in western Greece near the Albanian border, the closest airport to this town is located in Ioannina, roughly 80 kilometers distant.

The duration of the ferry transit from Igoumenitsa to Corfu is brief, typically around 1 hour and 20 minutes.

Fare rates for this route are reasonably priced, with passenger tickets typically ranging from 5 to 10.40 euros. Vehicle transportation incurs additional charges: 5 to 20 euros for motorcycles, 20 to 41.5 euros for cars, and 59 euros for camper vans.

The ferry operations between Igoumenitsa and Corfu are conducted by two companies: KerkyraLines and Kerkyra Seaways. These conventional ferries are sizable vessels equipped with indoor seating, open-air spaces, and vehicle storage capabilities. Designed to withstand adverse weather conditions, service interruptions or delays are infrequent. The interior sections of the ferries offer amenities such as climate control, television entertainment, and snack bars to ensure a comfortable voyage.

Accommodation Options

Delfino Blu Boutique Hotel

Delfino Blu Boutique Hotel is a distinctive and intimate establishment dedicated to providing a serene and health-focused retreat. Situated directly on the golden sands of Agios Stefanos Beach, the hotel offers an idyllic setting with crystal-clear waters and prime sunset views.

The ethos of the hotel centers on wellness, boasting modern spa amenities and facilities. Guests can unwind on the expansive beachfront or savor organic cuisine crafted from traditional recipes.

Accommodations at Delfino Blu are designed with comfort and elegance in mind, featuring bright spaces equipped with computers, flat-screen televisions, and DVD players. The spacious rooms include luxurious bathrooms complete with spa tubs and inviting seating areas with sofas.

A variety of room options are available, including superior studios with bay views, family studios, honeymoon suites, and garden-view suites, each offering a distinct perspective of the hotel's picturesque surroundings.

Renowned for its value, Delfino Blu provides exceptional service and high-quality organic products, delivering a sense of luxury without the premium price tag.

Advance reservations are recommended to secure preferred accommodations and potential discounts. While walk-ins may find availability, planning ahead ensures a confirmed stay.

The hotel's tranquil environment is perfect for those seeking relaxation and a connection with nature, set in a serene locale with breathtaking vistas.

However, those desiring a vibrant, urban atmosphere may find the hotel's tranquil setting less suitable. Delfino Blu caters to guests preferring leisure and tranquility.

Located in Agios Stefanos, the hotel is removed from the hustle and bustle yet remains within reach of Sidari's nightlife for those interested.

Accessibility to the hotel is straightforward, positioned on Agios Stefanos Beach and a manageable distance from Corfu Airport, with the hotel providing necessary directions.

Guests consistently praise Delfino Blu, evidenced by its flawless 5.0 rating from 918 reviews, solidifying its status as a premier travel destination.

The hotel accommodates various payment methods, ensuring convenience for all guests.

Inclusivity is a priority, with the hotel committed to facilitating a comfortable experience for guests with diverse needs.

Travelers are advised to verify the operational status of local attractions prior to visiting.

In terms of pricing, the hotel aligns with the upscale wellness market, reflecting the serene and opulent experience it affords.

Kerkyra Blue Hotel N' Spa

The Kerkyra Blue Hotel N' Spa offers a variety of activities to enhance your stay. Maintain your fitness routine in the well-equipped gym, savor a refreshing beverage at the bar, or relax in the inviting lounge area. Additional amenities include a picturesque garden, a tennis court, and an outdoor swimming pool for your enjoyment.

Each guest room serves as a comfortable sanctuary, complete with essential amenities such as air conditioning, a television, and a refrigerator. A kettle is provided for your morning coffee or tea, and the bathroom is fully stocked with necessary items.

Accommodation options cater to all types of travelers, from single rooms to luxurious sea-view rooms and expansive suites for those seeking extra space and comfort.

The hotel offers a balance of cost and convenience. While not the most economical option, the proximity to the beach and the array of on-site activities justify the investment.

For optimal rates, it is advisable to book your stay in advance. Last-minute bookings, particularly during peak seasons, may result in higher costs.

The hotel boasts an enviable location adjacent to the beach, complemented by a hospitable staff. With a 4.5-star rating, guests can anticipate a high-quality experience.

Guests who prefer more secluded environments may find the hotel busier than desired during the summer months.

The Kerkyra Blue Hotel N' Spais located in Corfu Town, the hotel is conveniently located a short

of an open-air cinema for movie enthusiasts to enjoy films beneath the stars. This ensures a diverse range of activities suitable for all preferences.

Accommodations at Ikos Dassia prioritize comfort, featuring rooms equipped with balconies to savor the views, air conditioning for the warmer days, and televisions for leisurely downtime.

Catering to various travel arrangements, the resort offers a spectrum of room options, from economical choices to luxurious suites, ensuring suitability for both solo travelers and groups.

While Ikos Dassia is not the most economical option in the vicinity, the comprehensive offerings and premium facilities provide substantial value, justifying the investment for many guests.

For optimal rates, it is advisable to secure reservations in advance through online booking platforms, mitigating the uncertainty of on-the-spot availability.

The resort's strengths include exceptional service from its staff and a plethora of dining experiences. However, those who prefer a less inclusive approach may find the resort's offerings excessive.

Located along the picturesque Dassia Bay, the resort promises stunning waterfront vistas.

Accessibility is straightforward, with a brief 20-minute journey from Corfu Airport leading directly to the resort.

Ikos Dassia accommodates various payment methods, ensuring a hassle-free transactional process for guests.

Inclusivity is a cornerstone of the resort, with specially designed accessible rooms available for guests with specific needs.

Potential visitors should note that certain attractions may be unavailable during the off-season, and it is recommended to verify operational status prior to arrival.

Ikos Dassia is a premium destination that, despite its higher price point, is considered by many to provide a worthwhile experience reflective of its cost.

Crystal Blue Barbati

Crystal Blue Barbati is a charming retreat that offers guests a sense of home away from home. Located in a tranquil area surrounded by olive groves, it provides a serene getaway from the daily grind. The property affords stunning ocean vistas, and Glyfa Beach is just a brief walk away, where visitors can enjoy the sunshine and sea.

The venue features an inviting pool for a refreshing dip, a sun terrace for ultimate relaxation, and a garden ideal for leisurely strolls. Guests can enjoy the convenience of complimentary WiFi throughout the premises.

The accommodations are thoughtfully equipped with kitchenettes for self-catering, and each room boasts a private balcony to savor the magnificent views. Air conditioning ensures comfort during warmer weather.

The studios are spacious and designed with comfort in mind, ensuring a welcoming atmosphere.

Crystal Blue is celebrated for its excellent value, offering clean and comfortable lodgings at an affordable price.

Booking in advance is advisable to secure a reservation and possibly benefit from better rates. While walk-ins are welcome, availability may be limited during peak seasons.

The property's location is exceptionally peaceful, and the family that operates it is renowned for their hospitality. Those seeking a lively nightlife or numerous activities might need to consider alternative accommodations.

Crystal Blue Barbati is situated in the picturesque area of Glyfa, Barbati, on Corfu, with convenient beach access. The most efficient way to reach the property is by car, with a short 20-minute drive from Corfu International Airport.

With a review rating of 4.5 out of 5, it's evident that guests have thoroughly enjoyed their stay. The property accepts various payment methods, making transactions effortless.

The establishment strives to be accessible to all guests, but it is recommended to contact them directly to ensure specific needs can be met. Local attractions' operational hours may vary by season, so checking in advance is prudent.

For precise pricing information, direct communication with Crystal Blue Barbati is suggested. Their contact details are readily available on their website, inviting guests to reserve their stay.

Oceanis Barbati

Oceanis Barbati offers a welcoming stay, infused with the charm of Greece. This idyllic retreat boasts a prime location where guests can appreciate the splendor of the Ionian Sea and feel an authentic connection to the local culture. Positioned to provide panoramic views, the apartments are an invitation to experience the natural beauty of the sea and verdant landscape.

The facilities at Oceanis Barbati cater to both leisure and connectivity. Guests can enjoy a swim in the pool with a sea view or stay up-to-date using the complimentary WiFi on the sun terrace under the Mediterranean sunshine.

The accommodations blend comfort with practicality. Each room features a kitchenette, ideal for preparing snacks or light meals. The private balconies are a personal haven for guests to relax and enjoy the scenic views.

Options include both studios and apartments, all designed with a focus on creating a tranquil and welcoming space. The decor is understated and appealing, contributing to a restful stay.

Visitors consistently commend Oceanis Barbati for its excellent value, noting the clean and comfortable lodgings, essential amenities, and memorable vistas.

Advance booking is recommended to ensure availability, particularly during the peak summer months. Although walk-ins may be accommodated, securing a reservation is advisable.

Situated near Glyfa Beach, Oceanis Barbati is a serene sanctuary, conveniently located a mere 20-minute drive from Corfu airport for those with vehicles.

The establishment enjoys a high guest satisfaction rating of 9.0 out of 10, reflecting its commitment to providing a high-quality experience.

Oceanis Barbati accepts various payment methods for a smooth transaction process. While the property strives to be accessible, potential guests should contact the establishment to discuss specific accommodations.

It's important to note that some local attractions may have seasonal operations, so checking their availability in advance is recommended.

Oceanis Barbati is an excellent choice for travelers seeking a peaceful Greek getaway at an affordable price point.

Getting Around Corfu

Exploring Corfu Town on Foot

Corfu Town, the principal city on the island, is recognized as a UNESCO World Heritage Site and is ideally experienced on foot. Visitors can wander through the historic streets, explore museums, and appreciate the distinctive architecture. Key attractions include the Old Fortress, the Archaeological Museum, and the Palace of Saints Michael and George.

For those preferring public transportation in Corfu, buses present an affordable and convenient choice. There are several bus services available:

1. Local Buses (Blue Buses): Suitable for brief journeys within Corfu Town and adjacent areas, including the airport and port.
2. Tourist Buses: Designed for sightseeing, these buses often provide hop-on, hop-off services at major tourist destinations.

3. Intercity Buses (Green Buses): Intended for longer distances, they connect Corfu Town with other locations on the island.

Luggage can typically be carried on local buses without an additional fee, provided it does not occupy excessive space. Similarly, intercity buses have luggage compartments, and no extra charge is applied if the luggage fits within the allotted space.

Travelers should be aware that delays are possible, particularly during peak periods. Most roads are well-maintained, but some rural routes may be more narrow or winding.

Fares for local buses start from €1.10 to €1.80 for short distances, while intercity bus fares range from €1.60 to €8, varying by destination. Journey times depend on traffic conditions and the distance traveled, so planning is advisable.

To board a local bus, signal the driver at any official stop. Intercity buses adhere to a timetable and can be boarded at bus stations or designated stops along their routes. For taxi services, ensure that the vehicle is officially licensed and equipped with a visible meter and rate card.

Carrying small change for bus fares is recommended, and travelers should verify any timetable changes before departure. Corfu's enchanting landscape awaits your discovery.

. Renting Vehicles

If you're thinking about renting a car in Corfu, it's a smart choice for getting around the island on your own schedule. Let me break it down for you in simple terms:

Choosing a Car to Rent:

Compact Vehicles: These vehicles are economical and ideal for solo travelers or couples. Their maneuverability makes them perfect for navigating narrow spaces.

Vehicles for Families: Designed for group travel, these vehicles provide ample space and comfort for extended journeys.

Convertible Cars: Ideal for those who appreciate the open air, these vehicles offer an unobstructed view of the scenery as you travel.

Car Rental Options

- Local Enterprises: These businesses often provide competitive rates and personalized service.

- Renowned Agencies: Established companies such as Europcar or Enterprise offer reliability and an extensive selection of vehicles.

Rental Locations
- Vehicles can be rented from numerous locations across the island, with the flexibility to return them at different designated spots.

Pricing and Operating Hours
- Rental costs start from approximately €13 per day, varying based on the vehicle model and rental duration.
- While most rental services operate during standard business hours, some may accommodate late arrivals.

Optimal Car Rental Venues
- Airports and Harbors: Renting upon arrival offers utmost convenience.
- Online Reservations: Pre-booking can lead to more favorable rates.

Identifying Reputable Rental Services
- Look for official signage and branding at their premises.
- A transparent contract and insurance options should be provided.

- Customer reviews online can be a good indicator of the company's reputation.

A note on driving in Corfu: The island's roads offer a unique driving experience with their serpentine layout and stunning vistas. Exercise caution while driving and enjoy discovering Corfu's attractions at your leisure.

This revised text avoids the specified words and maintains a professional tone, suitable for a broad audience. If you need further assistance, feel free to ask!

Group Tours in Corfu:

Sightseeing Tours: Join a guided bus or walking tour to visit the island's renowned attractions.

Maritime Excursions: Delight in scenic boat tours that include cave explorations and beach relaxation.

Adventure Outings: For the adventurous, there are off-road tours offering an adrenaline rush.

Tour Costs
Prices vary based on the tour type. Pedestrian tours may start at €25, while full-day boat excursions can exceed €50.

Tour Schedules

Tours typically operate during daylight hours, with most beginning at 9 AM and concluding by sunset. Evening tours are also available.

Booking Information

Tours can be conveniently booked online through platforms like Viator or TripAdvisor, allowing for price and option comparisons.

Alternatively, local travel agencies in Corfu offer in-person booking services, providing an opportunity to tailor your experience to your preferences and budget.

Transportation Options

Taxi and Private Car Services: These services offer convenient transportation across the island, including Corfu Town and secluded beaches.

Costs

Taxis: Base fare starts at €3.60, with an additional charge of approximately €1.10 per kilometer. Night fares may be higher.

Private Cars: Fixed prices are often provided upfront, varying by destination.

Operations

Taxis: Available 24/7, payment is made directly to the driver upon arrival.

Private Cars: Advance booking is recommended, especially during peak tourist seasons.

Payment Methods

Taxis: Cash payment is made to the driver.

Private Cars: Bookings and payments are processed according to company policies, typically via website or phone.

Locating Taxis

Taxi Stands: Located at the airport, seaport, and key areas in Corfu Town.

Hailing Taxis: Vacant taxis can be flagged down on the street.

Fare Calculation:Taxis use a metered system that calculates the fare based on distance traveled from a base rate.

Identifying Official Taxis:Official taxis are marked with a rooftop light, an internal fare meter, and a visible license plate.

Ensuring Accurate Fare:Always request a receipt as proof of payment and fare details.

Overcoming Language Barriers: Carry a written address or show it on your phone to aid communication with drivers who may not be fluent in English.

Boat Rental
Renting a boat offers a unique perspective of Corfu's coastline and secluded areas.

Remember, the best mode of transportation in Corfu will align with your personal travel style and accommodation location. Whether you choose public transit or a private service, there are diverse options to enhance your holiday experience.

PART 2:THINGS TO DO IN CORFU

Explore The Corfu Old Town

Corfu Old Town stands as a testament to the passage of time, offering visitors a window into the architectural and communal developments of ancient civilizations. Situated on the island of Corfu, adjacent to the sea, this historic town dates back to the 8th century BC. Its character has been shaped by the diverse cultures of Italy and England, among others, who have made it their home throughout the centuries.

Strolling through the narrow lanes of Corfu Old Town, one is greeted by towering structures with charming windows and doors that seem to leap out of a fairytale. The town boasts grand fortifications that once protected its inhabitants from marauders and invaders. Spianada Square, one of Europe's most expansive squares, serves as a central hub for locals and visitors alike. The town is peppered with an array of churches, museums, and a palace that once housed nobility.

For those lodging in Corfu, hotel personnel can provide the simplest directions to the Old Town. Given the proximity of many hotels, guests may opt to walk or take a short bus journey.

While some landmarks, such as the Old Fortress, require an admission fee of approximately 6 euros for adults, wandering the town and appreciating the exteriors of its historic buildings incurs no cost.

Travelers can feel secure in Corfu, with the usual precautions advised in any bustling locale. Comfortable shoes are recommended due to the extensive walking required to fully experience the town.

The distinctive feature of Corfu Old Town is its architectural fusion, a rare confluence of Greek, Italian, and British design elements from various periods.

Visitors to Corfu Old Town are encouraged to leisurely absorb the splendor of its age-old edifices, enjoy a leisurely coffee in the square, and ponder the extensive history that has transpired there. It is a place that conveys stories from a bygone era, inviting you to contribute to its ongoing story.

Liston Promenade

The Liston Promenade, established during the French sovereignty of the island in the 1800s, is a testament to historical elegance and architectural diversity. Designed by a French engineer to evoke the grandeur of Paris, the promenade's name derives from the Italian 'Liston', signifying a broad, linear avenue.

As one strolls along the promenade, the sophisticated design of the buildings unfolds, featuring arches that confer an air of nobility. The architectural style is a distinctive fusion of French, Venetian, and British elements, offering a unique visual experience.

Located conveniently within Corfu Town, the promenade is adjacent to the expansive Spianada Square, a venue known for hosting cricket matches and serving as a communal gathering space.

While there is no charge for enjoying the promenade's ambiance, visitors may find that dining or indulging in refreshments at the local establishments comes at a premium due to the area's popularity.

For tourists, Corfu maintains a reputation for safety, yet vigilance is advisable in crowded locales to safeguard personal items.

The Liston Promenade invites exploration and leisure, boasting edifices with historical military significance and cafes that offer traditional Greek coffee among other delights. Visitors are encouraged to capture the beauty of the arches and buildings through photography. The evening hours, illuminated by ambient lighting, enhance the promenade's charm, inviting guests to linger and savor the atmosphere.

In essence, the Liston Promenade is more than a mere thoroughfare; it is a corridor through time, offering an immersive historical experience. Visitors are encouraged to fully engage with the environment and create lasting memories.

Corfu Archaeological Museum

The Corfu Archaeological Museum offers a profound journey through antiquity, presenting a collection of artifacts that illuminate the lives of individuals from millennia ago. Established in the 1960s, the museum initially served as a repository for relics unearthed at the Temple of Artemis in Corfu. Over time, it expanded to encompass a broader array of discoveries from Corfu's ancient locales, providing insights into the historical lifestyle of its inhabitants.

Visitors to the museum can marvel at significant exhibits such as the Gorgon Pediment, an imposing stone sculpture that once guarded the temple, and the Lion of Menecrates, a symbol of fortitude. The collection also includes ancient currency, implements, and even playthings that offer a glimpse into the quotidian existence of past eras.

Located conveniently within Corfu Town, the museum is readily accessible on foot from most local accommodations and via public transportation from the central bus station.

Admission fees are modest, with adult entry priced at approximately 4 euros, granting access to a remarkable array of historical treasures.

While Corfu is recognized for its hospitality and security for visitors, it is always prudent to exercise vigilance over personal belongings.

The Corfu Archaeological Museum is distinguished by its exhibition of diverse historical styles and periods. Each artifact contributes to the overarching narrative of historical human existence.

As you traverse the museum, take the time to contemplate each exhibit thoughtfully, considering the historical narratives they represent. The museum serves as a conduit to the past, offering an enriching experience in historical discovery.

Spianada Square

Spianada Square, located at the core of Corfu, Greece, stands out as one of the largest squares within the nation and Europe. This expansive area serves as a cherished gathering place for both residents and visitors to unwind, socialize, and bask in the sunlight. The square's name, "Spianada," derives from the Italian term for "flattening," a nod to the Venetian's clearing of the land in the 1500s to fortify the city.

For those residing in Corfu Town, reaching Spianada Square is a breeze due to its central position. A simple stroll will suffice. For guests staying at more distant locations, public buses and taxis offer convenient transportation options, with buses being the more economical choice and taxis providing a quicker alternative.

The square boasts an abundance of trees and seating, offering a tranquil spot for relaxation. It's not uncommon to find individuals engaging in cricket on the expansive lawn. Encircling the square are various cafes and eateries, presenting ample opportunities for dining or enjoying a beverage.

While there is no charge to explore the square, visitors planning to patronize the surrounding cafes or stores should be prepared to spend, as the prices tend to be elevated in this sought-after locale.

Corfu maintains a reputation for being safe for tourists, yet it remains prudent to stay vigilant of personal belongings and surroundings, particularly during peak times.

The essence of Spianada Square lies in its harmonious fusion of historical architecture and contemporary life. The ancient structures coexist with the vibrant present-day activities, offering a genuine glimpse into the spirit of Corfu for both locals and tourists alike..

New Fortress

The New Fortress in Corfu, known as Fortezza Nuova, is a historical marvel constructed by the Venetians between 1576 and 1645 on St. Mark's hill. This fortress served as a protective barrier for the town, reflecting the value placed on the island's safety.

For those residing in Corfu Town, the fortress is a pleasant walk away, offering an opportunity to appreciate the local ambiance. Visitors staying farther can opt for public transportation or a taxi for convenience.

Admission to the New Fortress is complimentary, allowing everyone to explore without a fee. At the summit, there's a delightful café where guests can unwind and enjoy the scenery.

Corfu is generally safe for tourists, but it's wise to be vigilant. Pay attention to personal items and surroundings, particularly in crowded areas.

The interior of the New Fortress promises an exciting journey. Guests can admire the ancient architecture and the breathtaking views of the town and sea. The ascent may be demanding, but the vistas from the top are rewarding, particularly during the early morning or evening.

The New Fortress is not merely an old edifice; it is a gateway to the past. Its blend of historical importance and scenic allure makes it a unique destination, where one can sense the historical echoes of its former defenders.

PART 3. DISCOVERING CORFU'S BEACHES

Paleokastritsa Beach

Paleokastritsa Beach, renowned for its pristine waters and scenic beauty, stands as a gem on Corfu Island.

Legend has it that this locale is where Odysseus came ashore and encountered Nausicaa. The moniker 'Paleokastritsa' suggests the proximity of an ancient fortress, specifically Angelokastro, which bears witness to the island's historical conflicts.

Visitors lodged in Corfu can reach Paleokastritsa Beach via bus, taxi, or personal vehicle. The bus fare is economical, approximately €2.30 per journey. Taxis offer a faster alternative, though at a higher price ranging from €30 to €60. For those preferring independence, car rentals are available.

The beach itself invites guests without charge. However, amenities such as sunbeds or umbrellas incur a fee. Adventurous visitors may explore nearby caves by boat, with tickets costing about €10-15 per individual.

The area is generally secure for tourists. Vigilance over personal belongings is advised, and caution is recommended due to the terrain's incline and numerous steps.

Attractions to Explore:
- Varied beaches, some sandy and others pebbled, offer relaxation.
- The historic Paleokastritsa Monastery, perched atop a hill, provides breathtaking panoramas.
- Coastal cave tours are available by boat.
- Local cuisine can be savored at beachside eateries.

Its allure lies not only in its natural splendor but also in its storied past and mythological associations. Visitors can swim in the luminous waters, enveloped by the mystique of ancient Greek lore.

Visitors are encouraged to leisurely enjoy the sun and the enchanting atmosphere of Paleokastritsa Beach, creating lasting memories of their time on Corfu Island.

Glyfada Beach

Originally a tranquil coastal area, Glyfada Beach has transformed into a vibrant seaside destination. Celebrated for its fine, golden sands and shallow, calm waters, it offers the perfect environment for sunbathing and swimming.

Visitors lodging in Corfu can take a bus directly to Glyfada Beach, with an approximate travel time of 45 minutes and a fare ranging from €1 to €3. Alternatively, a taxi can provide a quicker journey of around 17 minutes, though at a higher cost of about €30 to €40. For those with personal vehicles, driving is also an option.

Enjoying the beach itself incurs no charge, but rentals for sunbeds and umbrellas are available for a fee. Additionally, water sports such as jet skiing and parasailing are offered for those seeking thrill, each with respective costs.

While Glyfada Beach is generally safe, vigilance over personal belongings is advised. Protective measures against the sun, including the use of sunscreen and adequate hydration, are essential, particularly during peak heat.

Activities and Amenities

- Visitors can relax on the soft sand or opt for rented sunbeds for enhanced comfort.
- The pristine waters invite guests for a refreshing swim.
- A range of water sports is available for the adventurous.
- A selection of eateries and bars provides convenient access to food and beverages along the beachfront.

Glyfada Beach offers more than a typical beach experience; it's a lively and beautiful setting that promises memorable moments under the Greek sun, surrounded by the sea.

Agios Gordios Beach

The beach derives its name from the Saint Gordios church, a prominent feature on the beachfront. Originally a tranquil village locale, it has transformed into a bustling tourist spot.

Visitors in Corfu can reach Agios Gordios Beach by bus, taxi, or personal vehicle. Buses provide an economical mode of transport, while taxis offer a direct route at a higher fare of approximately

€30-€40. For those driving, parking facilities are available free of charge.

Enjoying the beach itself incurs no charges. However, renting a sunbed or umbrella entails a nominal fee. Additionally, engaging in water sports will require payment.

While Agios Gordios is generally secure for vacationers, it is advisable to monitor personal belongings and remain vigilant of sea conditions, particularly when participating in water sports.

Attractions and Activities:
- Relax on the beach or swim in the sea.
- Try out water sports such as paddleboarding or windsurfing.
- Explore surrounding trails for stunning views of the island.

Agios Gordios Beach is distinguished by its beautiful natural environment complemented by convenient amenities, offering a harmonious blend of rustic Greek charm and modern facilities.

Visitors to Agios Gordios Beach can expect to be impressed by the scenic views, enjoy local cuisine at beachside restaurants, and find the location's charm enhances their holiday experience. The beach caters to both tranquility and adventure, making it a versatile destination for all types of travelers.

Sidari Beach

Sidari Beach is known for its pristine sandy shores and inviting atmosphere, making it an ideal destination for sunbathing, aquatic activities, and relaxation.

Originally a quaint fishing locale, Sidari underwent a transformation in the 1980s. The development of hotels and restaurants infused life into the area, attracting tourists. Notably, the beach features the Canal D'Amour, known for its breathtaking cliffs and secluded bays. Local folklore suggests that a swim through the canal could lead to finding one's soulmate.

Visitors in Corfu can take a bus to Sidari Beach, which is approximately an hour away and costs a few euros. Alternatively, a taxi offers a faster option, though it is more expensive, ranging from €70 to €85. Driving is also a viable option for those who prefer it.

The beach itself is free to enjoy. However, renting a sunbed or umbrella incurs a fee of about €7 to €10.

Additional charges apply for those interested in watersports or boat tours.

While Sidari is generally safe, visitors should remain vigilant with their possessions and exercise caution during swimming and watersport activities.

Activities at Sidari Beach:
- Unwind on the soft, sandy beach.
- Swim in the Canal D'Amour and possibly meet a special someone.
- Engage in thrilling activities such as jet skiing or parasailing.
- Explore the local shops and savor the cuisine at beachside restaurants.

Sidari Beach's unique charm lies in its blend of stunning landscapes, a variety of activities, and a friendly atmosphere, ensuring memorable experiences for all who visit.

Canal d'Amour

The Canal d'Amour, situated on Corfu Island, is a hidden treasure where nature's grandeur is on full display through unique rock formations and the sea's deep blue shades.

Dubbed the "Channel of Love," this site is renowned for its stunning natural beauty and the romantic legends associated with it. According to lore, couples who sail through the canal will have everlasting love. The sandy cliffs have been shaped by the sea and wind over time into extraordinary shapes that captivate today's visitors.

From your accommodation in Corfu, you can take a bus, taxi, or drive to the Canal d'Amour. The bus is economical and takes about an hour from Corfu's center. Taxis are faster but costlier. If driving, parking is available nearby.

Access to the Canal d'Amour is free, but dining at nearby restaurants will incur charges. Prices may be higher due to the convenience and views.

The area is generally safe for visitors, but caution is recommended, especially when swimming or climbing the rocks. Be mindful of your footing and surroundings, especially during busy times.

Attractions and Activities
- Walk along the cliffs to enjoy the breathtaking sea views.

- Swim through the canal to fulfill the local legend.
- Relax on the small beach and soak up the sun.
- Visit nearby sites like Cape Drastis for additional impressive scenery.

What Sets It Apart:
The Canal d'Amour is more than just a beach; it's a remarkable place where history, legend, and beauty converge. It captures the hearts and ignites the imaginations of all who visit.

PART 3: CULTURAL AND NATURAL ATTRACTIONS

Achilleion Palace

The Achilleion Palace, stands as a testament to history and architectural grandeur. Constructed in the 1890s by Empress Elisabeth of Austria, affectionately known as Sisi, the palace served as her sanctuary, a place of solace from her life's tribulations, chosen for its breathtaking landscapes and her affinity for the lore of ancient Greece.

For those residing in a Corfu hotel, a direct bus service to Achilleion Palace is available. The journey lasts approximately 24 minutes and is economically priced between €1 and €2. Alternatively, a taxi can provide a more personal travel experience, reaching the destination in about 11 minutes, with fares ranging from €21 to €25. Self-drivers will find it a brief 10-kilometer drive to the palace.

Adult visitors are required to pay an entrance fee of approximately €7, with reduced rates applicable for children and students. The palace welcomes visitors daily from 08:00 to 20:00, offering ample time for exploration.

While Corfu is generally a safe destination, vigilance with personal belongings is advised, along with adequate hydration, particularly during the warm summer months.

Attractions:
- Visitors can admire the palace's striking architecture and its exquisite gardens, adorned with statues depicting Greek mythology's deities and heroes.
- The famed statue of Achilles and the panoramic vistas of Corfu from the palace's elevated positions are not to be missed.
- The interior is equally captivating, with rooms furnished with artworks and artifacts narrating the palace's storied past and its inhabitants.

Achilleion Palace is more than a historical edifice; it was the brainchild of a historical figure deeply enamored with Greek culture. It stands as a unique confluence of Austrian and Greek heritage, offering visitors an authentic experience of this cultural synthesis.

Mount Pantokrator

Mount Pantokrator, the highest peak on Corfu, rises to an impressive 906 meters. From its summit, visitors can enjoy panoramic views of the island and, on clear days, glimpse Albania. The peak's name, translating to 'all-powerful' in Greek, reflects the majestic experience of standing atop this mountain.

Originally known as Istoni, Mount Pantokrator has been a significant site since 1347 when a monastery was established there in honor of Jesus Christ, supported by local communities. Although it suffered destruction in 1537, the current structure dates back to the late 17th century, with renovations adding a new façade in the 18th century.

Visitors can reach the peak by navigating the winding roads from the coastline or by trekking up the mountain. The journey typically begins in the south, passing through the villages of Spartilas and Strinilas en route to the summit. The approach route varies depending on one's starting point in Corfu, often involving travel from the northeast coast inland.

There is no admission fee to visit Mount Pantokrator. However, a café located at the summit offers refreshments at reasonable prices, complemented by breathtaking views.

Due to the intense sunlight at high elevations, it is advisable to apply sunscreen and wear a hat, particularly for those hiking. The ascent involves numerous sharp bends, which may affect individuals susceptible to motion sickness. It is essential to wear appropriate footwear and carry water.

Attractions:
- The Monastery of Pantokrator provides a serene space for contemplation.
- The summit offers expansive vistas of Corfu and beyond.
- Old Perithia, Corfu's oldest village, is nestled on the mountainside.
- The summit café invites visitors to relax and enjoy local delicacies.

Mount Pantokrator is a site of profound historical and cultural significance, offering a tranquil retreat from the bustling coastal resorts. The fresh, high-altitude air provides a serene atmosphere for visitors.

In visiting Mount Pantokrator, it is recommended to take one's time, breathe in the pure air, appreciate the silence, and fully absorb the extraordinary landscape. Such an experience promises to be memorable, long after returning to lower elevations. Enjoy your exploration of this remarkable mountain.

Mon Repos Palace

Mon Repos Palace, a site of significant historical importance and natural allure, is located on the island of Corfu. This location serves as a confluence of historical resonance and scenic beauty.

Built in 1828, Mon Repos Palace was originally the summer retreat for the British Lord High Commissioner of the Ionian Islands. After the union of these islands with Greece in 1864, it transitioned into a residence for the Greek royal family. It is also known as the birthplace of Prince Philip, the Duke of Edinburgh.

Currently operating as a museum, Mon Repos Palace extends an invitation to visitors to explore its collection of Corfu's historical artifacts, which includes items like ancient ceramics and statuary.

The palace is surrounded by vast gardens that provide a peaceful environment for leisurely walks and relaxation.

The museum charges an approximate fee of 4 euros per person for entry. The gardens, however, are accessible without any charge.

Corfu is acknowledged as a safe travel destination. Visitors should take care to safeguard their belongings and stay hydrated, especially during the hot season.

From any Corfu hotel, visitors can choose between a taxi or a bus to get to Mon Repos Palace. A taxi ride is quick, about 4 minutes, costing between 8 to 10 euros. The bus, while more affordable, may take a bit longer to reach the destination.

Experiences and Activities at Mon Repos Palace:
A visit to Mon Repos Palace allows you to:
- Explore the museum and learn about Corfu's extensive history.
- Enjoy the calm atmosphere of the gardens, which feature a variety of plant life.
- Take in the sweeping views of the Ionian Sea from the palace's position on Analipsis Hill.

Mon Repos Palace stands as a gateway to the grand history and the rich narrative of Corfu. It offers a retreat where visitors can connect with historical periods amidst the island's enchanting environment.

Corfu Old Fortress

The Old Fortress of Corfu, situated on the eastern flank of Corfu town, stands as a testament to history's enduring legacy.

Constructed initially in the 6th century for rudimentary defense purposes, the fortress underwent significant expansion by the Venetians in the 15th century to fortify against maritime invaders and other hazards. It boasts two conspicuous elevations and is encircled by a moat, transforming it into an island-like stronghold.

For those residing in Corfu town, a leisurely stroll to the fortress is possible, with the route graced by the allure of historic edifices. Visitors lodging at a distance may opt for public transportation or a taxi service.

Entry to this historical marvel is granted for a fee of approximately 6 euros—a modest sum for the breathtaking vistas and historical richness that lie within.

Corfu is largely secure, yet vigilance over personal items is advised. Comfortable walking shoes are recommended, as the visit entails considerable walking and stair climbing.

The interior of the fortress reveals a church, reminiscent of a Greek temple, erected by the British. Ascending to the lighthouse is encouraged for its magnificent, sweeping views. The pathways within the fortress are the very ones once guarded by soldiers.

The Old Fortress is more than a mere collection of ancient structures; it is a living chronicle, offering vistas of the sea unchanged since the time of its original sentinels.

Visitors are encouraged to allocate ample time for exploration. Standing by the sea, feeling the breeze, one can contemplate the myriad souls who have shared this vantage point through time. It is an authentic journey into another epoch and a profound adventure. Enjoy your exploration to the fullest!

This revised passage avoids the specified terms and adheres to a professional writing standard, ensuring originality and compliance with Amazon's guidelines.

Angelokastro Castle

Angelokastro, known as the "Castle of Angels," is a historic fortress perched atop a steep cliff on Corfu's northwest coast. Established to protect the island from invasions, it has stood the test of time. Along with two other fortifications, it formed a defensive network across Corfu.

For those residing in a Corfu hotel, Angelokastro is accessible by bus or taxi. The bus is economical but slower, whereas a taxi offers a quicker journey at a higher cost. Self-drivers will find parking available near the castle.

Entry to Angelokastro is a modest €3 per person, granting access to a site brimming with historical intrigue.

The ascent to the castle requires sturdy footwear due to uneven terrain, and carrying water is advisable for hydration. While the area is safe, caution is recommended.

Visitors to Angelokastro can explore the ancient walls and a charming church dedicated to Archangel Michael at the peak. The sweeping views of the sea and surroundings are stunning.

Angelokastro's significance lies not only in its longevity but also in its ability to connect visitors with the past, offering vistas once surveyed by its guardians.

In your exploration of Angelokastro Castle, allow ample time to absorb the atmosphere and reflect on its historical significance. This experience promises to be a memorable part of your Corfu visit.

PART 4: ENJOYING LOCAL CUISINE AND ACTIVITIES

Traditional Corfiot Dishes

To truly experience Corfu, one must delve into the local cuisine, which offers more than mere sustenance; it provides a gateway to the island's heritage.

Consider Pastitsada, a robust pasta dish served with a zesty tomato sauce and meat such as veal or rooster. Taverna Laopetra in Benitses serves an excellent version of this dish from 12:30 PM to 11:00 PM daily, with prices ranging from 10 to 20 euros.

Sofrito is another must-try, featuring beef simmered to perfection in a white wine and garlic sauce. Avalle Bistro in Kommeno Bay is renowned for this dish, available from noon until midnight each day, priced between 15 to 30 euros.

For seafood enthusiasts, Bourdeto offers a fiery fish stew seasoned with red pepper and herbs. Aegli

Restaurant, located in Liston Square, Corfu Town, is the ideal spot for this dish, serving from morning till night, with main courses priced between 15 and 25 euros.

These dishes are a celebration of Mediterranean flavors, abundant in spices and island-grown ingredients like olives and lemons. Dining on these specialties is akin to a journey through Corfu's history.

For those staying in Corfu Town hostels, the central market is easily accessible for further culinary exploration. It's an excellent venue for sampling additional local delicacies and discovering the island's diverse agricultural and artisanal products.

Olive Oil Tasting

In Corfu, the exploration of olive oil is a delightful experience. Here are some notable destinations where you can savor the authentic flavor of local olive oil:

The Governor's Olive Mill: This establishment serves as a conduit between traditional and contemporary methods of olive oil production.

Visitors are invited to explore the historical process of making olive oil and discover the reasons behind the superior quality of their product. The mill is open for tours nearly every day, with operating hours from 9 AM to 8 PM on weekdays and 9 AM to 1 PM on Sundays.

Corfu Olive Oil Museum: Operated by the Mavroudis family, this museum occupies a historic stone structure formerly used as an olive mill. The museum offers an informative journey through the history of olive oil production, from the 1500s to present-day techniques. It is a unique opportunity to witness the progression of olive oil manufacturing. The museum welcomes visitors from Monday to Saturday, 9:45 AM to 6 PM.

Villa Posillipo Corfu: At this venue, guests can embark on a culinary exploration, sampling various types of extra virgin olive oil, including some that have garnered accolades in Corfu. These exquisite oils are served alongside freshly baked bread and regional delicacies.

A visit to these sites offers more than just olive oil tasting; it is an introduction to the cultural heritage and historical practices of olive oil production in Corfu. Enjoy your journey through the flavors and narratives of Corfiot olive oil.

Water Sports And Outdoor Activities

Parasailing at Sidari Beach

Participants are hoisted into the air via parachute, providing an exhilarating perspective of the island akin to an aerial map, delivering a sense of liberation

Location: Sidari Beach
Availability: Daily, 9 AM to 7 PM
Cost: Approximately €40 for a single ascent

Jet Skiing at Barbati Beach

Riders can expect an adrenaline-fueled journey across the waves, juxtaposed with moments of tranquility amidst the ocean's expanse.

Location: Barbati Beach
Availability: Daily, 10 AM to 6 PM
Cost: Starting at €30 for a 15-minute session

Kitesurfing at Chalikounas Beach

The Kite Club offers instruction in kitesurfing, a sport that combines surfing with kite flying, ensuring a thrilling experience for novices and seasoned surfers alike, complete with necessary equipment.

Location: Chalikounas Beach

Availability: Schedule upon request

Cost: Lessons begin at approximately €70

Windsurfing at Issos Beach

Ideal for surfing aficionados, the club provides all necessary gear for a fulfilling windsurfing experience, supported by favorable wind conditions.

Location: Issos Beach
Availability: Inquire for details
Cost: Varied pricing for equipment rental and lessons

Sailing with No Stress Yachting

A serene sailing venture, allowing for exploration of secluded areas and enjoyment of the crystalline waters, epitomizing a tranquil exploration of Corfu

Location: Marina Gouvia
Availability: Contact for information
Cost: Full-day excursions start at approximately €400

For those residing in hostels and eager to explore these offerings, consider renting a scooter for independent navigation of the island. Alternatively, the local green buses present an eco-friendly transport option. Each activity presents an opportunity to create lasting memories and gain insights into the rich heritage and culture of Corfu. Embrace the aquatic adventures and allow each wave to contribute to your narrative of discovery on this enchanting island.

Nightlife in Corfu

Corfu offers a diverse array of nocturnal activities catering to various tastes. Here is an overview of some premier destinations for evening entertainment and how to enjoy them:

The Boathouse Bar & Cocktails: This establishment provides an idyllic setting by the sea, ideal for enjoying a beverage as the evening sky displays a spectrum of colors. Situated on the periphery of Roda, it is conveniently reachable via a brief taxi journey from most local accommodations. Currently operational, visitors are welcome to schedule their visits at their leisure.

Maria's Famous Karaoke Fun Pub: A hub of merriment and melody, this pub invites both locals and tourists to partake in a night of spirited singing. Centrally located within Corfu's vibrant nightlife district, it is accessible by taxi or public transportation.

The Fountain Coffee Cocktails & More: Positioned in Kavos, this venue is the perfect starting point for an evening out, renowned for its hospitable staff and delectable fare. Proximity to most hotels in Kavos allows for an easy transition into the night's festivities.

Vintage Cocktail Bar: Offering a tranquil setting, this bar is ideal for guests seeking a more subdued evening. It boasts an extensive cocktail menu and is easily reached by public transport or a short commute from Corfu Town.

The Vine: Connoisseurs of wine will be delighted by The Vine, a wine bar exuding a distinctive charm and offering an exquisite wine selection. As a somewhat secluded spot, it is best accessed by taxi.

These venues collectively represent the vibrant essence of Corfu's nightlife. From bustling bars and spirited karaoke to serene cocktail lounges and refined wine bars, the island promises memorable experiences for every visitor. It is advisable to verify current operating hours and prioritize safety while reveling in the nightlife.

Shopping for Local Crafts and Souvenirs

Corfu offers an authentic shopping experience that reflects the island's vibrant culture and creativity. Below is an overview of some notable shopping destinations:

Corfu Town Main Market

A bustling marketplace offering an array of fresh fruits, vegetables, seafood, and spices. It's an ideal place to purchase local specialties such as olive oil and honey.

Location: Centrally situated in Corfu Town.

Operating Hours: Open from morning to early evening, with the recommendation to visit in the morning for the freshest produce.

Price Range: Variable, with opportunities to find excellent deals on local products.

The Land Of Corfu Natural Products

Specializes in natural products, including herbal beauty items crafted from olive oil and kumquat. A prime spot for unique, locally-made gifts.

Location: Located at Filarmonikis 25 Ag. Spyridonos in Corfu Town.

Operating Hours: Open daily from 9 AM to 10 PM.

Price Range: Reasonably priced for premium local merchandise.

Sweet 'N Spicy Bahar Shop

A haven for culinary enthusiasts, this shop features an assortment of spices, Greek wines, liqueurs, and homemade jams, all sourced locally.

Location: Situated in the capital of Corfu.

Operating Hours: Aligns with standard shop hours.

Price Range: Affordable, offering high-quality spices.

Patounis Soap Factory

More than a shop, it's an interactive experience where visitors can witness traditional soap-making processes.

Location: A historic establishment in Corfu Town.

Operating Hours: Visit their website or contact them directly for current hours.

Price Range: Economical.

Meandros Gold

Offers exquisite jewelry that encapsulates Greek heritage, perfect for a memorable souvenir.

Location: Found throughout Corfu, particularly in main shopping areas.

Operating Hours: Adheres to regular shopping hours.

Price Range: Somewhat expensive, reflecting the authenticity of the jewelry.

Liston Promenade

The promenade exudes a European charm with its array of shops offering everything from local handicrafts to high-end apparel. It's also a pleasant locale for a coffee break and people-watching.

Location: Adjacent to Spianada Square in Corfu Town.

Operating Hours: Shops typically open from 10 AM to 10 PM.

Price Range: Diverse, catering to various budgets.

Old Town's Narrow Alleys

The alleys are lined with small boutiques showcasing handmade jewelry, olive wood carvings, and leather goods, set against a backdrop of vibrant local life.

Location: A labyrinth of streets behind the Old Fortress.

Operating Hours: Generally from 9 AM to 8 PM.

Price Range: Mostly economical, with numerous artisanal shops.

Corfu's Local Artisan Shops

These boutiques are treasure troves of authentic Corfiot art, featuring items like hand-painted ceramics, textiles, and paintings, each with its own narrative

Location: Scattered throughout Corfu Town.

Operating Hours: Usually from 9 AM to 9 PM.

Price Range: Fair for handcrafted items.

Makrades Village

Renowned for its regional specialties such as herbs, olive oil, and honey, Makrades provides a glimpse into the rural traditions of Corfu.

Location: Nestled in the mountains of northwest Corfu.

Operating Hours: Daytime hours, varying by shop.

Price Range: Attractive prices for the quality offered.

Kanoni Peninsula Shops

These trendy boutiques offer locally-made clothing and souvenirs that capture the essence of Greek island life, complemented by scenic views.

Location: In proximity to the renowned Kanoni viewpoint.

Operating Hours: Typically from 10 AM until sunset.

Price Range: Slightly higher due to the tourist-centric location.

Accessing these markets from your accommodation is straightforward, with options to take a local bus or rent a bike for a scenic route. Each location offers a distinct slice of Corfu's charm, so savor the experience. Wishing you a delightful shopping journey in Corfu!

Festivals And Event

Corfu, the Greek island, is renowned for its dynamic festivals, each steeped in history and brimming with life.

The Corfu Carnival: A fusion of local traditions and Venetian influences, the carnival transforms Corfu Town into a spectacle of color and satire. The festivities peak in early spring, particularly on the first Sunday of Lent and the preceding Sunday.

Easter Celebrations: More than a religious observance, Easter on Corfu is a communal cultural phenomenon. The entire island partakes in age-old customs, with Corfu Town hosting the most elaborate spectacles during Easter weekend.

Varkarola in Paleokastritsa: This summer event celebrates the sea with illuminated boats, fireworks, and choral renditions of local melodies. The bay of Paleokastritsa becomes an enchanting scene, typically during a full moon in August.

The Festival of Saint Spyridon: Honoring the island's patron saint, this festival occurs several times a year, blending devotion with local customs. The processions through Corfu Town's streets occur on Palm Sunday, Easter Saturday, the first Sunday in November, and December 12th.

The Olive Festival: Paying tribute to Corfu's olive cultivation heritage, this festival features traditional music and dance, offering a taste of the island's olive produce. It's held in the olive-growing villages, usually in the autumn following the harvest.

Visiting these festivals offers an authentic glimpse into the heart of Corfu, showcasing its traditions, the warmth of its people, and their celebratory spirit. Each festival promises unique experiences filled with memorable sights, sounds, and tastes, ensuring that the island's vibrant spirit leaves a lasting impression on all who partake.

Conclusion

As we conclude our journey through Corfu, we reflect on the myriad experiences we've cherished. This guide aimed to be a companion, guiding you through the serpentine alleys, the verdant groves of olive, and the tranquil shores of this enchanting isle.

Corfu transcends a mere destination; it's a mosaic of stories, crafted by diverse cultures, radiating sheer beauty. From the venerable fortifications guarding the Old Town to the genial taverns that extend a warm welcome with each repast, this island etches itself into your memory.

Parting with Corfu, carry with you the resplendent sunsets that drape the Ionian Sea, the mirthful moments savoring kumquat liqueur, and the serene interludes beneath the cool canopy of a time-honored olive tree. These recollections will serve as a reminder of the time you stepped away from the hustle of life to embrace tranquility.

Corfu doesn't bid farewell; it offers a promise of return. It beckons you to revisit, to explore the undiscovered and to return to the places that resonated like home. As this guide reaches its conclusion, consider Corfu's narrative as one that continues, awaiting your return to further its chapters.

Thank you for allowing this guide to accompany you on your Corfiot escapade. May your future voyages continue to be a source of inspiration, wherever they may lead. Journey forth with care, and may our paths cross again in the near future, dear traveler.

Printed in Great Britain
by Amazon

42387828R00050